Flowers

FOR CAKE DECORATING

By L. J. Bradshaw

MEREHURST
LONDON

Published 1990 by Merehurst Limited
Ferry House
51-57 Lacy Road
Putney
London SW15 1PR

© Copyright 1990 Merehurst Limited

ISBN 1-85391-155-0

All rights reserved. No part of this publication may be reproduced, stored in a retrieval system, or transmitted in any form or by any means, electronic, mechanical, photocopying, recording or otherwise, without the prior written permission of the copyright owner.

Edited by: Barbara Croxford
Designed by: Jerry Goldie
Cover photography by: Ian Copping
Typesetting by: Angel Graphics, London
Colour separation by: Spectrum Reproductions, Colchester
Printed in Belgium by Proost International Book Production

Contents

Introduction	4	Wedding designs	23
Using the book	5	Wedding designs	24
Tracing		Wedding theme	25
Pin-pricking		Wedding flowers	26
Sugarcraft techniques		Wedding designs	27
Arranging flowers	6	Christening flowers	28
Formal arrangements		Floodwork cake tops	29
Informal arrangements		Floral side designs	30
Making a start		Cake board designs	31
Planning your floral design		Floral runout collars	32
Arranging flowers	7	Floral collar overlays	33
Designing and making		Four seasons	34
Important details		Happy Valentine	35
Flowers using cutters	8	Mother's Day	36
Floodwork flowers	9	Easter flowers	37
Stems and fillers	10	Christmas	38
Leaves and foliage	11	Garlands and wreaths	39
Arrangements	12	Vases and baskets	40
Layouts for round cakes	13	Men's flowers	41
Flowers for square cakes	14	Corner designs	42
Layouts for oval cakes	15	Flowers for stencilling	43
Daisy	16	Floral lettering	44
Fuchsia	17	Floral numerals	45
Rose	18	Flower faces	46
Lily of the valley	19	Buttercream flowers	47
Engagement flowers	20	Buttercream designs	48
Piped lace pieces	21		
Orchid	22		

Introduction

Flowers and cake decoration go hand-in-hand and have been used extensively by the confectioner for hundreds of years. In the early days, edible flowers for use on cakes were beautifully formed from various edible media such as royal icing, sugarpaste, chocolate and cream. With the advent of much commercially produced confectionery, the trend went towards using mass-produced wafer flowers, plastic flower cake decorations and more recently silk and fabric flowers.

When the sugarcraft boom started a few years ago, flower modelling took on a new look with many different ideas in the creation and application of floral work being introduced. Many of the so-called new flower making techniques stemmed from those existing methods, being adapted and improved upon by the many new, talented and creative sugarcraft artists. Like all other aspects of sugarcraft, it has been researched and developed until flower modelling has become a specialized area of sugarcraft work. New equipment, special pastes, cutters, tools and techniques have all played a vital role in the success of flower crafting for cake decoration.

Flowers for Cake Decorating has been specially designed to meet the exacting requirements of the modern cake decorator, providing an extensive library of patterns, templates and floral reference. Simple explanations of the more popular flower making techniques are included. However, the object of the book is to offer a wide and varied range of flowers, leaves and stem templates, together with numerous complete arrangements, layouts and borders, to be used on celebration cakes for all occasions.

Following the success of *Patterns*, *Lettering* and *Stencilling*, this fourth title in the series – *Flowers for Cake Decorating* – complements the other titles, and makes an invaluable addition to the sugarcrafter's bookshelf providing an extensive library of reference. The book is suitable for both beginners and advanced sugarcraft artists, and offers many simple designs to get you started, together with more intricate ideas for the more experienced cake decorator. While the book reflects the current interest in flower craft by sugarcraft artists, inspiration from these pages will no doubt be found by embroiderers, designers, poster writers and flower arrangers, and will appeal to them as an invaluable source of reference and new ideas.

Enjoy your flower arranging!

Best wishes   Lindsay John Bradshaw

Using the book

Hand-crafted flowers used by cake decorators can be made from royal icing, marzipan, sugarpaste, chocolate, buttercream and even rice paper. There are also a number of non-edible flowers which have become more and more popular, especially for commercial use, over the past years. They include fabric, silk, plastic and dried flowers – all widely available from a variety of outlets such as florists, craft shops and of course sugarcraft suppliers. Although non-edible flowers can be purchased and used as suggested to attractively decorate cakes, the aim of this pattern book is to stimulate and inspire you to make and create flowers from various edible media using different sugarcraft methods and techniques, then to decoratively arrange them on your cake creations. Hand-crafted work is far more satisfying to the person working it and doubly satisfying when the cake can be given as a gift expressing a personal and caring touch.

This book is very easy to use, just follow a few simple guidelines as you use the individual themes of each page to provide single blooms, sprays, side designs, full cake tops and many more examples of floral work to suit cakes for every occasion.

A book devoted entirely to patterns and templates will inevitably feature numerous references to tracing, pin-pricking and flower making techniques. To avoid repetition, the various methods are described on this page. Simply refer back to this section as required.

Transferring the design

To re-create the design of your choice from the book, you will need to trace the image from the page. Using good quality tracing paper or greaseproof (waxed) paper, place the paper over the design and outline carefully and neatly including all the necessary detail. Use an HB pencil sharpened to a good clean point for accurate reproduction.

Tracing

To transfer the design onto paper for say a cake side template, turn the tracing over and outline the design using an HB pencil again, reverse the tracing once again and place into position on the paper. Finally outline with a slightly harder pencil, such as a 2H, to give a crisp line.

To transfer the design directly onto a cake, use the pin-prick method described below.

Pin-pricking

Trace the design of your choice from the page as described above. Instead of reversing the tracing to re-outline it, place the tracing on the iced surface taking care not to smear any unsightly pencil marks. Secure the tracing temporarily if required with a small piece of masking tape. Now simply follow the design with a fine pointed tool, mapping pen or similar implement to transfer a dotted image onto the icing. Make the dots as close or distant as you require to make a recognizable outline. Do not, however, press into the icing too much as this could result in large holes which may prove difficult to disguise when employing certain techniques to produce your flower designs.

Sugarcraft techniques

A brief description of the more popular sugarcraft techniques suitable for flower making are described below.

Painting

The same techniques used for painting scenes, figures and animal motifs on cakes and plaques can be successfully used to paint very attractive floral pictures. Mix edible food colours, paste or liquid with an edible white confectioner's compound to make the paint. Outline the design of your choice, then use various tints and shades to produce life-like flowers and leaves.

Cut-out

This type of flower makes a quick and easy decoration for gâteau and celebration cakes. It is also ideal for beginners to lead them into more advanced floral techniques. A step-by-step method is featured on page 8.

Floodwork

A popular method of producing decoration for many types for cakes. The floodwork technique can be used for chocolate and piping jelly work as described on page 9 or for royal icing runout work, see pages 9, 29, 32 and 42.

Royal iced flowers

Piped full-relief A small square or circle of waxed paper on which to pipe the flower is placed on a flower nail. Using a special petal piping tube (nozzle), single petals can be piped in formation to create a full flower. The flowers can range from flat type flowers like primroses and violets through half-relief ones like daffodils with trumpets and sweet peas with overlapping petals, and even three-dimensional full flowers like roses. After drying, the flowers are peeled away from the waxed paper and used in arrangements. Attach the flowers to the cake top with tiny dabs of royal icing. The same technique can be used to make buttercream flowers (see page 47).

Piped half-relief Using tube (nozzle) Nos1 and 2, bulb, petal and teardrop shapes are piped in sequence to form full flowers. A small centre bulb completes the flower and represents the stamen. This type of flower may be piped on waxed paper to be used as required for decoration, or they can be piped directly onto a cake top, side or prepared plaque.

Stencilling

A step-by-step method of this technique is provided on page 43.

Brush embroidery

A technique used predominantly for floral designs but equally useful for animal and figure work. A line of royal icing is piped to form an outline, which is then brushed inwards while still soft. An addition of clear piping-gel to the icing will delay the drying process, thus giving more time to work the design accurately.

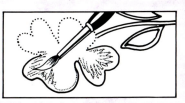

Tube embroidery

A method of reproducing various embroidery stitches in icing. Fine tubes (nozzles) are used with various appropriately coloured icing to pipe satin stitch, chain stitch, cross stitch, running stitch and many many more. Beautiful floral work can be accomplished using this technique. Pipe directly onto a sugarpaste, royal iced or chocolate surface.

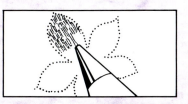

Designing a circular flower

To obtain a more consistent shape within the design of a flower, you can combine geometric principles and the techniques of tracing. Most open flowers can be based on a circle, if the circle is then divided into the number of petals required, each segment can be used to contain a drawing or outline of a single petal. To form an accurate flower drawing, repeat the petal shape in the remaining segments by tracing.

Arranging flowers

Strict rules are not required when arranging flowers for cake decoration. An arrangement or layout that looks attractive and appeals to one person may look totally wrong to another. All that is necessary are a few simple guidelines to follow.

To spend too much time arranging and fixing, flowers can result in an arrangement that looks 'over-worked', making an over-fussy and not too pleasing an effect. A simple, natural look is the one to aim for, whether you want to produce a formal or informal look.

Formal arrangements

This type of arrangement will be governed to some extent by an imaginary outline shape, maybe a triangle, a crescent or an oval. Or the arrangement may take on a symmetrical design, being the same on both sides of a dividing line. Formal arrangements are useful for centring on a cake top or on a more 'fixed' type of overall cake design.

Formal   **Informal**

Informal arrangements

Informal arrangements are more difficult to achieve than formal ones as there are no real rules to adhere to such as geometric principles. Therefore, the design takes on a more loose appearance with plenty of naturally flowing curved effects being allowed to take over. Having said this, informal does not mean untidy – spend as much time as you feel necessary to create a relaxed, total look to the finished work.

Informal arrangements are built up by eye appeal, by the sugarcraft artists appreciation of the materials being used, the positioning, and also the occasion for which the flowers are intended.

Making a start

First try to visualize the effect you are trying to achieve – get ideas and inspiration from the complete designs and patterns featured in this book.

Unlike arranging fresh or dried flowers, you will probably have to create your own stem shapes for your 'designed' flowers rather than relying on the ready 'shaped' stems of fresh flowers. It is generally more difficult to achieve a natural flowing look with straight stems, so select curved and flowing type stems to begin with – straight stems create a more formal, rigid look. This, incidentally, is utilized quite considerably in cake decoration for some side designs, corners or where a real symmetrical look is required.

The form and arrangement of stems will sometimes be governed by the shape of the cake top and space available on it. A round or oval cake for instance will lend itself particularly well to curvy type groupings, whereas layer or bar cakes can carry straight stems easier – square cakes will accept both curved and straight. This is not a strict rule to adhere to, more a guide until experience is gained, as any shape of stem can be used on any shape of cake and still produce excellently balanced designs.

Generally it is better to use a limited range of flowers, rather than take one of each to produce your design, at least to begin with until you become more experienced at working with and combining varieties. The exception to this is if you are making a mixed posy, or collection of say summer blooms, where a wide range of colours and shapes is utilized.

Planning your floral design

Listed here are a few easy-to-follow guidelines to help you plan your design:

- Always take into account the type of surface on which the flowers are going to be used – royal icing, sugarpaste, chocolate, marzipan, buttercream etc.

- Give much consideration to the occasion for which the cake is intended, this will have enormous bearing on the selection of flowers. Is it a wedding, birthday, anniversary, man's cake etc?

- Assess the size of the cake – how big or small does the arrangement need to be?

- Decide upon your colour scheme for the background, ie the icing, sugarpaste or it is a dark brown chocolate covering!

- Select the type of flowers and determine the size required. Do you require flowers of an equal size or a mixture of small, medium and large.

- Select the background material, leaves and stems, and some foliage for the sides of the arrangement, ensuring that the stems curve the correct way for their position within the arrangement.

- When you have selected the flowers for the front of your arrangement, you may simply need a few fillers to complete the look.

- Use flowers of different heights so that the shorter ones can be used in front of the taller ones to hide the stems.

- Do not overcrowd arrangements, leave some space and 'air' between each flower and the leaves.

An equal number of flowers used in the arrangement.

A more natural grouping is achieved by using an odd number of flowers.

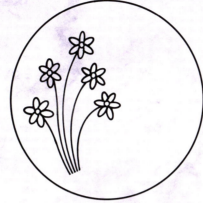

After arranging the stems, take care to position the flowers as naturally as possible, and not all on the same plane. This applies to both natural and imaginary flowers. To explain this, below are two flower arrangements, one with all the flowers on the same horizontal plane and the other more acceptable naturally arranged type of grouping, using varying levels or heights for each flower.

All flowers arranged on same level or plane.

Using similar curved stems but arranging the flowers on varying levels results in a more natural and informal appearance.

Using the same plane or level for each flower is sometimes inevitable on most segmented type cakes, such as a layer cake and large gâteau. An alternative method of arrangement would be to vary the flower levels on alternate segments.

Two design layout techniques widely used by the sugarcraft artist can be seen here being used to display flowers as a decorative theme.

Design repetition
The same design in each division of a segmented layer cake.

Design alternation
Segmented layer cake with two alternating sectional designs.

Designing and making

Having taken into account the various elements that need to be considered in planning your floral design listed on the previous page, give a little thought to the next stages of designing – Flower Colours, Leaves and Foliage.

Flower colours

These range from the palest tints through to very strong and rich, deep colours. Flowers are natural colours and therefore are generally acceptable to the human eye. In this respect the sugarcraft artist needn't worry too much about possible lack of harmony when using vivid colours, except in extreme instance of combination – even then they can be successfully incorporated into a design. The reason being we accept these natural colours as belonging to the flowers themselves and not to the cake itself.

Bear in mind the occasion the cake is intended for, the sex of the recipient and any other factors that may govern choice of pale, pastel or deep flower colours, such as the colour of bridesmaids' dresses to be used on a wedding cake.

Leaves and foliage

These should be studied carefully before attempting to use them in floral decoration. There are long narrow leaves belonging to the daffodil, iris and tulip type flowers, then there are the oval leaves of rose and fuchsia, the former 'group' of leaves being without veins, the latter having veins.

Study also leaf edges which vary tremendously – the plain, some with serrated edges and also the deeply cut and divided types – not to mention the various outline shapes. Leaf joints to main stems should also be noted to make them look right. This awareness will result in near botanically perfect reproductions on your cakes – if that is what you are aiming for! Of course, many cake decorators are happy to produce a pleasing, colourful group of flowers on a cake without becoming involved with all the intricacies – create your own 'designer' flower and leaf ideas. There is lots of scope for imaginary flowers if you prefer – you won't be copying nature so you can afford to bend the rules a little!

Important details

Here are a few helpful suggestions to ensure success with your arrangements:

- Use a selection of flowers in various stages of 'growth', such as tight buds, semi-open flowers, three-quarter open flowers and fully opened ones.
- Use flowers of different lengths and avoid placing flowers of the same height next to each other – have an up and down effect, rather than all the blooms on the same level or plane.
- Use flowers of different heights so that the shorter ones can be used in front of the taller ones to hide the stems.
- Group flowers in different shapes as a 'thread' running through an arrangement rather than all in one 'clump' with leaves as an unattractive 'collar' around them.
- After selecting your flowers and when arranging them, grade the flowers according to size and colour. Use the largest and darker coloured flowers towards the centre with the paler, smaller ones at the edges.
- All the stems should radiate from one central point, rather than positioned irregularly like a 'pin cushion'. Use curved flowing stems at the sides.
- Do not overcrowd arrangements, leave some space and 'air' between each flower and the leaves.
- The number of flowers used will be governed by the area of available space in proportion with the size of the cake top or side, the size of each individual flower and whether any other decoration is to be incorporated within the design, such as a name or inscription. Whatever the eventual total number of flowers is, a more natural appearance will be achieved by using the nearest odd number. Exceptions to this occur on equally numbered segmented gâteaux or layer cakes.

How to make flowers using cutters

As these flowers are cut out, they are made from sugarpaste or marzipan. Thinly roll out the paste.

Using a metal food cutter or knife, cut out circles, diamonds, ovals, squares, hearts and triangle shapes.

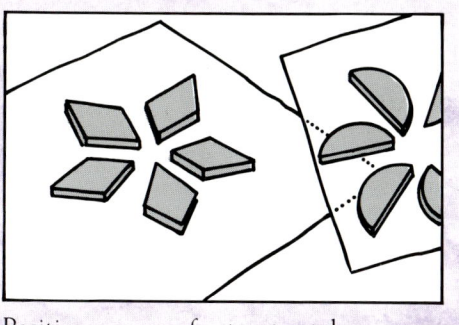

Position a group of cut-out petals on waxed paper. Alternatively, arrange directly onto the cake top.

Pipe a bulb of coloured royal icing in the centre of the flower to secure the petals and form the stamen.

Flowers using cutters

Quick and easy to make, requiring only the minimum amount of equipment, these simple yet very attractive flower decorations can be used to enhance celebration cakes, gâteaux and even small fancy cakes.

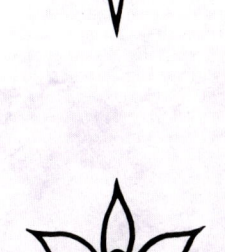
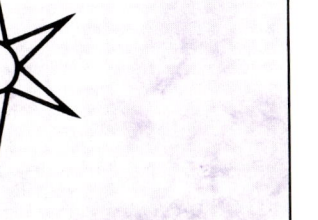

Piped chocolate flowers and leaves

Using a paper piping bag fitted with a No2 tube (nozzle), pipe out the shapes illustrated below with piping (thickened) chocolate.

Some shapes, such as the two-toned leaves, may be flooded-in with melted chocolate – try a plain chocolate outline flooded-in with milk chocolate.

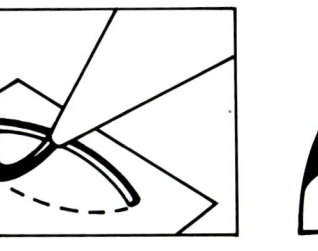

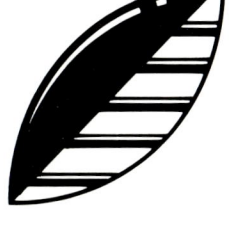

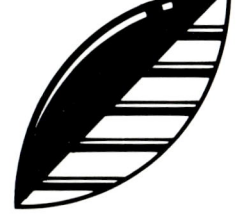

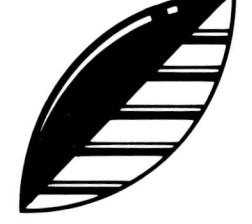

How to pipe jelly floodwork flowers

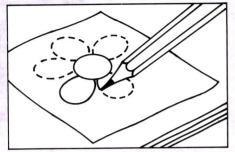

Make a tracing of the design required onto greaseproof (waxed) paper as described on page 5.

Place the tracing onto the sugarpaste-covered or royal-iced cake and pin-prick the outline onto the surface.

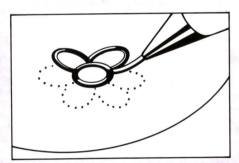

Outline the complete flower shape using a No1 or No2 tube (nozzle) with piping (thickened) chocolate.

Using a small piping bag, flood-in the petals, centres and leaves with brightly coloured piping jelly.

Circular garland for cake top

Floodwork flowers

A selection of outline designs ideal for run-icing floodwork techniques, but equally attractive when carried out in chocolate and coloured piping jelly. The designs are also suitable for other sugarcraft techniques.

Stems and fillers

Natural looking stem configurations can be difficult to achieve. Here's a useful selection of single and grouped stems, together with some 'fillers', with which to complete your arrangements.

Leaves and foliage

Here's a variety of leaves and foliage that can be accomplished using various sugarcraft techniques and materials. Use the leaves on their own or in conjunction with other designs in the book. For botanically correct designs, match the leaves to the correct flowers.

Arrangements

Achieving a pleasing balance of flowers, stems and leaves in an allocated space on differing shaped cakes can be quite daunting to a beginner. These six examples give some ideas of how to create an attractive overall appearance. Use these as a basis for developing your ideas as you progress.

Use the circles on the stems as a guide to the proportion, size and position of flowers.

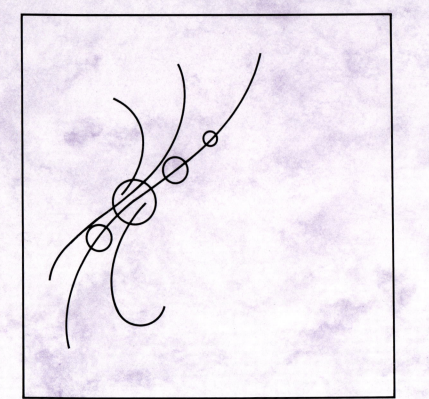
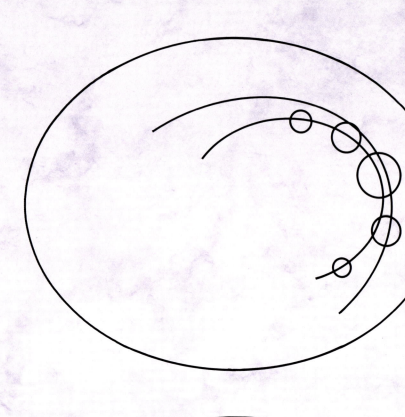
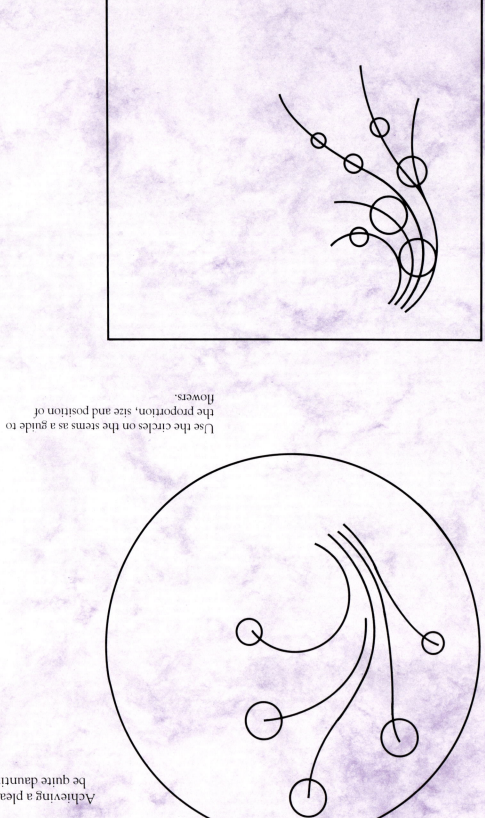
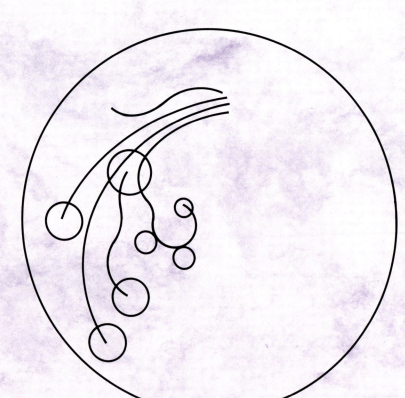
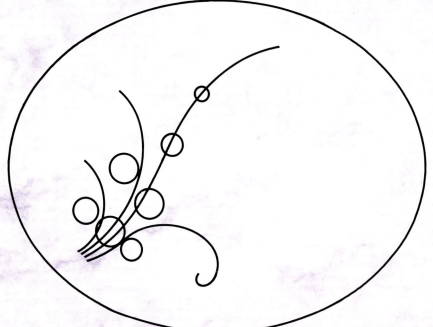

12

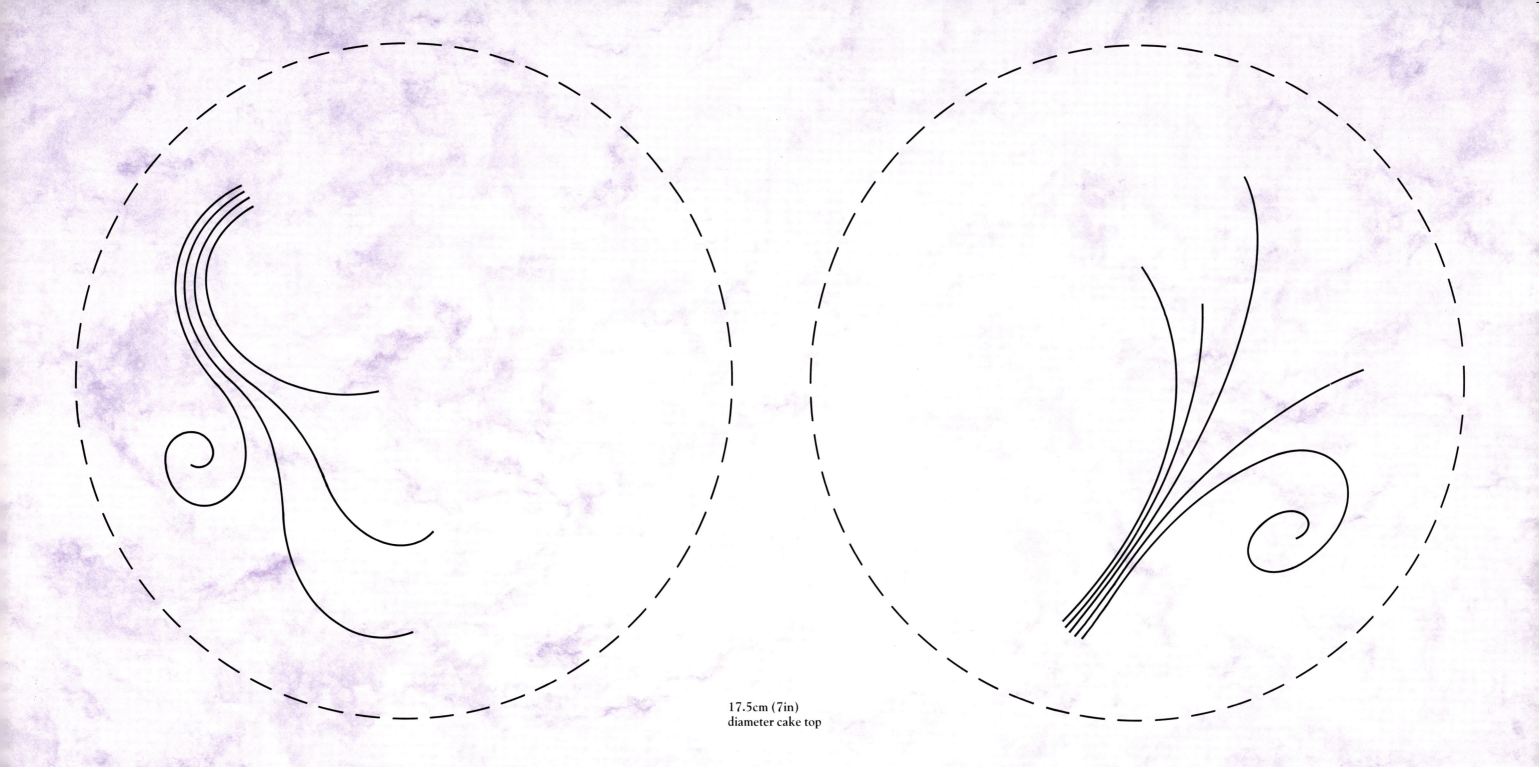

17.5cm (7in)
diameter cake top

Layouts for round cakes

Here are two examples of well balanced stem arrangements ideally suited to round cakes. With a little care and attention, the layouts could easily be adapted to suit cakes of differing shapes.

Flowers for square cakes

Making good design use of corners and straight edges is essential when planning decoration for square cakes
– here are two nicely balanced examples. Use the same basic design and alter the flowers to suit your theme,
in this way you can create several design options from a basic idea.

17.5cm (7in)
square cake top

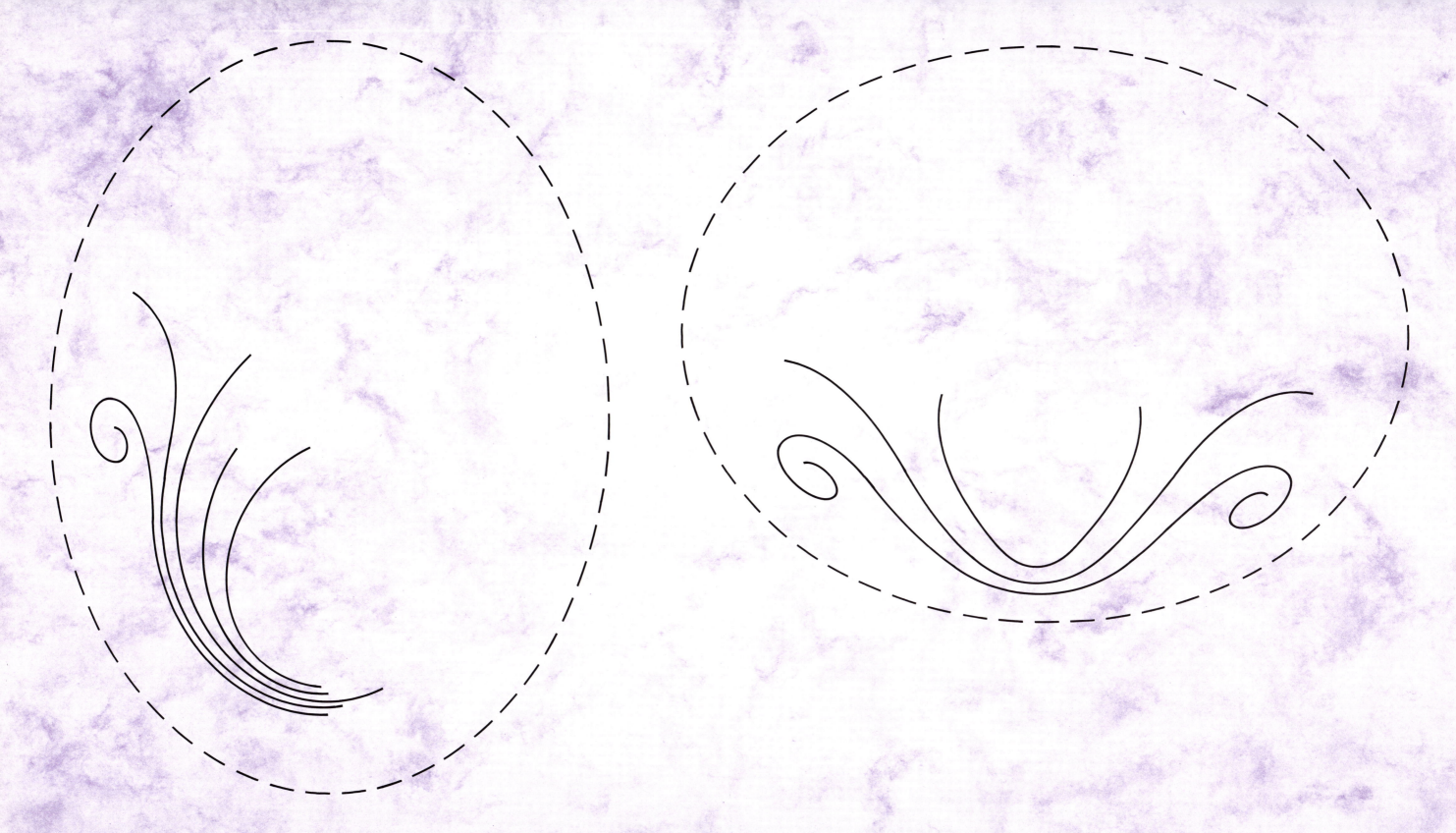

Layouts for oval cakes

The modern trend towards different shaped cakes gives the sugarcraft artist lots of scope to design beautifully flowing arrangements. Oval cakes are especially inspirational as can be seen here.

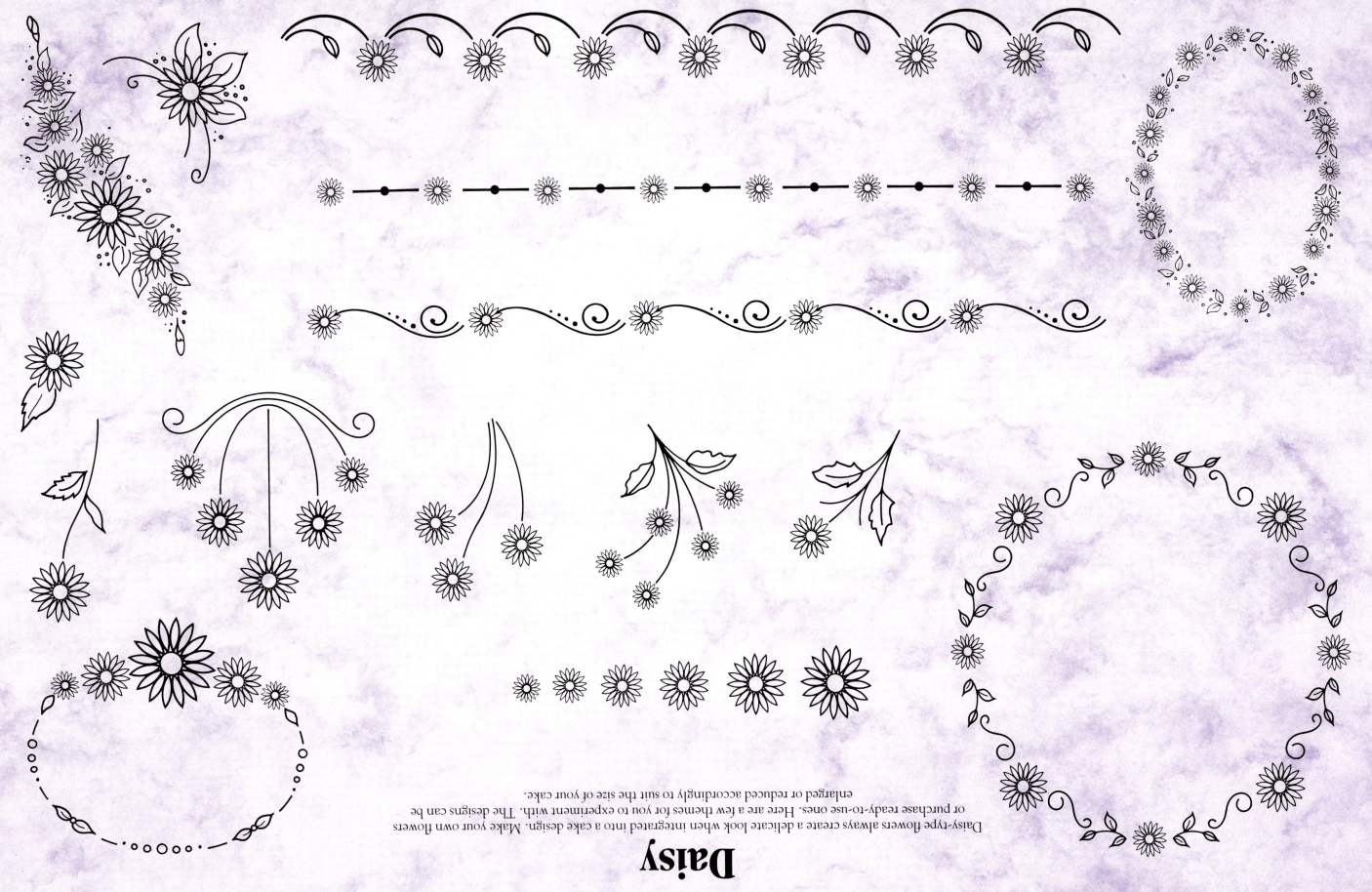

Daisy

Daisy-type flowers always create a delicate look when integrated into a cake design. Make your own flowers or purchase ready-to-use ones. Here are a few themes for you to experiment with. The designs can be enlarged or reduced accordingly to suit the size of your cake.

How to make a cut-out fuchsia

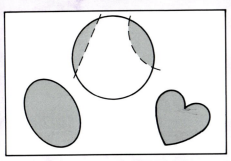
Prepare shapes as shown from thinly rolled out sugarpaste or marzipan in appropriate colours.

Assemble as shown directly onto the cake top or side, attaching together with water or a little royal icing.

Pipe the stamen as shown using royal icing with a fine tube (nozzle), such as a No0 or 1.

Complete the flower with the heart shape, then pipe on a thin stem using green-coloured royal icing.

How to work a fuchsia

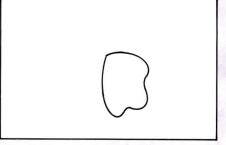
Whichever medium you choose to work in, always start with the basic shape of the petals (*corolla*).

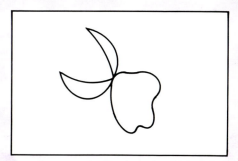
In order to create depth to the flower, the next stage is to work the distant sepals.

Using a fine tube (nozzle), pipe the stem (*pedical*), then add the foreground sepals and further work to complete the petals.

Finally add the ovary (stem joint) and pipe the stamen using a fine tube (nozzle), such as a No0 or 1, in a suitable colour.

Fuchsia

The beautiful fuchsia is somewhat neglected as a flower for cake decoration. With the stunningly subtle colour combinations and 'lively' appearance of the blooms, fuchsias make an ideal subject to enhance your cakes.

Rose

Probably the most well liked flower of all time, the rose in many various forms has long been associated with cake decoration. Suitable for making in numerous edible media, the rose will find a place on many of your sugarcraft creations.

Circular rose garland for cake top

Graduating sizes for multi-tiered cakes

How to pipe lily of the valley

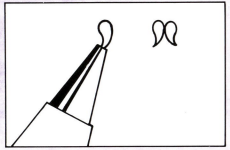

Method One
Use a fine piping tube (nozzle) with white royal icing or buttercream.

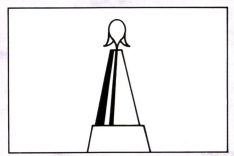

Over-pipe the two petals with a third larger pointed bulb shape to complete the flower.

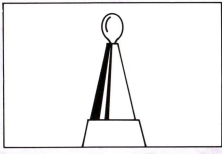

Method Two
Pipe a bold bulb shape with a point on the end, using a No1 tube (nozzle).

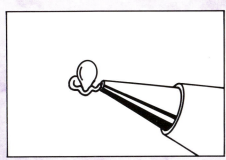

Using a finer tube (nozzle), pipe a curvy, scalloped-type line as shown for the petal edges.

Painted leaf arrangement – apply direct to cake top or plaque.

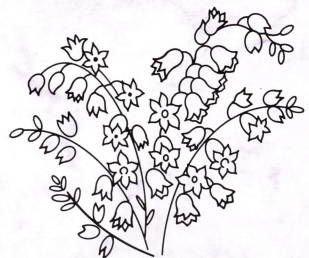

Align this flower template over the leaf template using the cross for accuracy. The stems and flowers are piped using white and green royal icing.

See page 43 for a lily of the valley stencil design.

Lily of the valley

This delicately beautiful miniature flower is usually associated with wedding cakes, but looks equally at home as a decoration on other special occasion cakes. Various sugarcraft techniques can be used for most of the designs shown here.

Engagement flowers

The romantic effect required for engagement cakes can often be difficult to achieve. The designs provided here use complementary floral work to enhance traditional engagement motifs.

17.5cm (7in) diameter cake top

17.5cm (7in) square cake top

How to pipe lace pieces

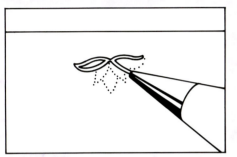

Place long narrow strips or small squares of waxed paper over the design of your choice.

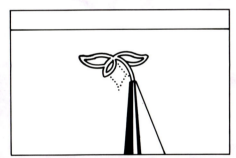

Commence piping, usually from the base of the lace piece, using a fine tube (nozzle) and fresh royal icing.

Continue piping as shown, building up the detail until the shape is complete. Proceed with the next piece.

Complete the required number of shapes. Allow to dry, then carefully remove from the paper and attach to the cake.

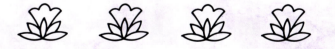

Piped lace pieces

Finely piped lace pieces make the perfect decoration for any sugarpaste-covered celebration cake; they also look equally attractive when used on royal-iced cakes. This comprehensive selection of designs has been specially created with a floral theme in mind.

Orchid

The beautiful orchid bloom is always associated as a wedding flower. A few attractive spray arrangements, together with a cake top and side design, provide much inspiration for the creative sugarcraft artist. Try orchids in brush embroidery – they are exquisite!

Piped line design

Cake line

Cake side template

Wedding designs

A varied selection of flower and leaf motifs provide endless scope for wedding cake decoration. The motifs can be used as side 'fillers' on both sugarpaste-covered and royal-iced cakes.

Wedding designs

Side panels on wedding cakes will look most attractive with the inclusion of these dainty floral designs and rose sprays. The designs are provided in graduating sizes for use on multi-tiered cakes.

Wedding theme

This simple design makes a delicately attractive floral theme for a bride cake, but it is equally useful as a decoration for other special occasion cakes, such as anniversary and birthday. (Illustrated on the front cover.)

25

Wedding flowers

Here is a selection of popular flowers usually associated with weddings. Magnolia, lily, freesia and dainty blossom are amongst those featured.

Wedding designs

These flower and leaf motifs are ideal for decorating the sides of a cake and also for piped detail on runout collars. The designs are provided in graduating sizes for use on multi-tiered cakes.

Christening flowers

Traditional christening motifs combined with floral embellishments provide delicate designs which can be adapted for a boy or a girl's christening cake. Simply make the design in an appropriate colour usually associated with this special occasion, namely blue for a boy, pink for a girl or lemon for either sex.

17.5cm (7in) square cake top

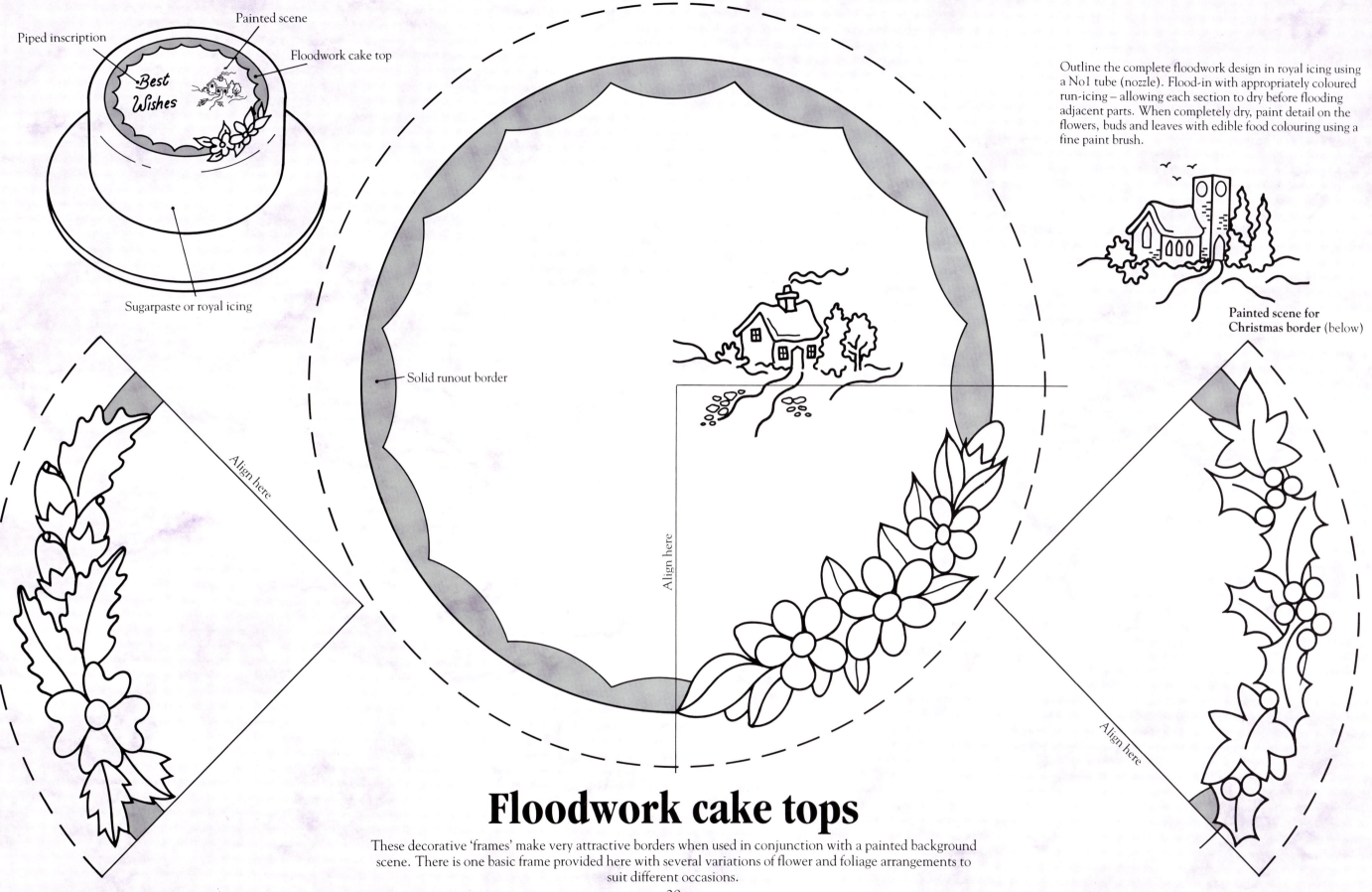

Outline the complete floodwork design in royal icing using a No1 tube (nozzle). Flood-in with appropriately coloured run-icing – allowing each section to dry before flooding adjacent parts. When completely dry, paint detail on the flowers, buds and leaves with edible food colouring using a fine paint brush.

Painted scene for **Christmas border** (below)

Floodwork cake tops

These decorative 'frames' make very attractive borders when used in conjunction with a painted background scene. There is one basic frame provided here with several variations of flower and foliage arrangements to suit different occasions.

How to make a cake side template

Wrap a strip of greaseproof (waxed) paper around the iced cake, measuring and marking where necessary.

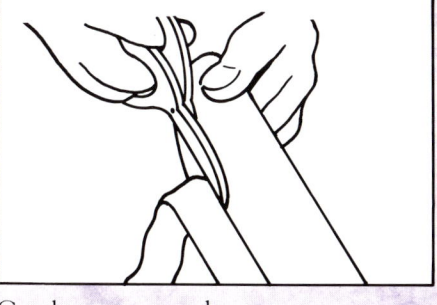

Cut the paper to make an accurate template the depth of the side of the cake.

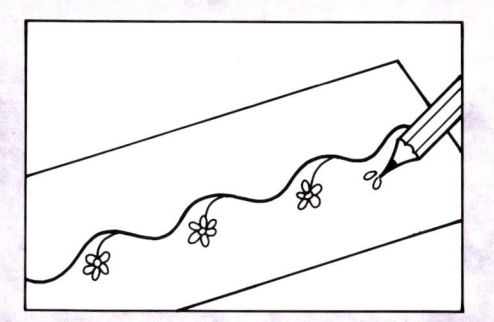

Trace the cake side design of your choice onto the paper directly from the page.

Secure the template to the cake side with masking tape. Pin-prick the design ready for piping or painting.

Floral side designs

The sides of cakes can quite often be difficult to design. Here are a few ideas that can be mixed and matched to suit the main design theme of your cake. Simply use the basic framework of the patterns provided and change the flowers to suit.

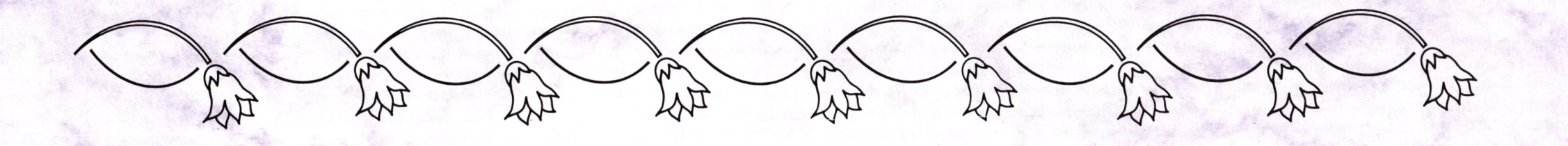

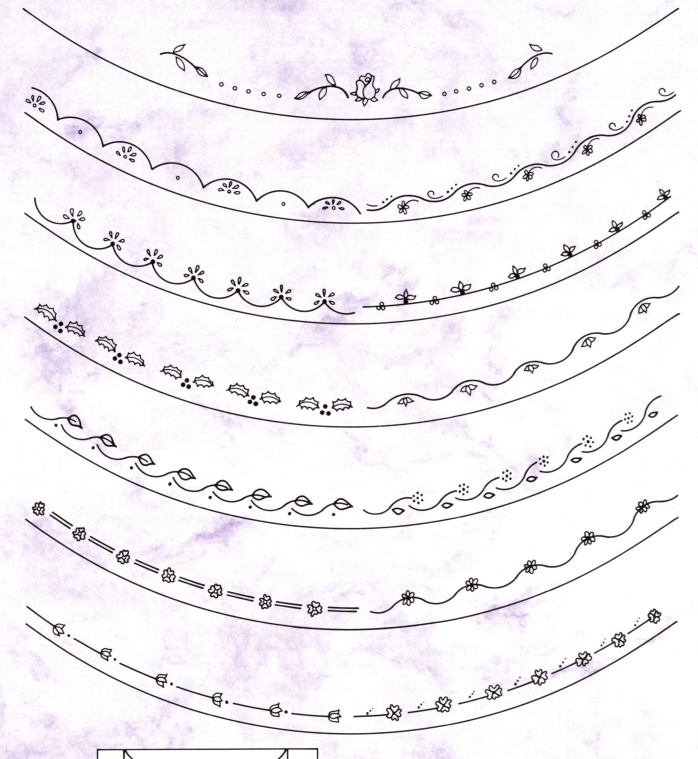

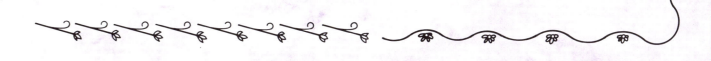
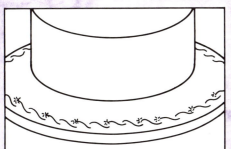
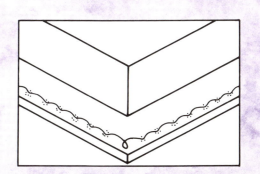

Cake board designs

Instead of simply edging your cake board with ribbon or a band, why not utilize the space to add further complementary decoration in the form of these dainty floral line designs. Try coordinating the board decoration with the main theme of your design.

Floral runout collars

Runout collars as a border decoration add an extra dimension to both royal-iced and sugarpaste-covered cakes. The patterns provided here combine traditional cake design with attractive and varied floral themes.

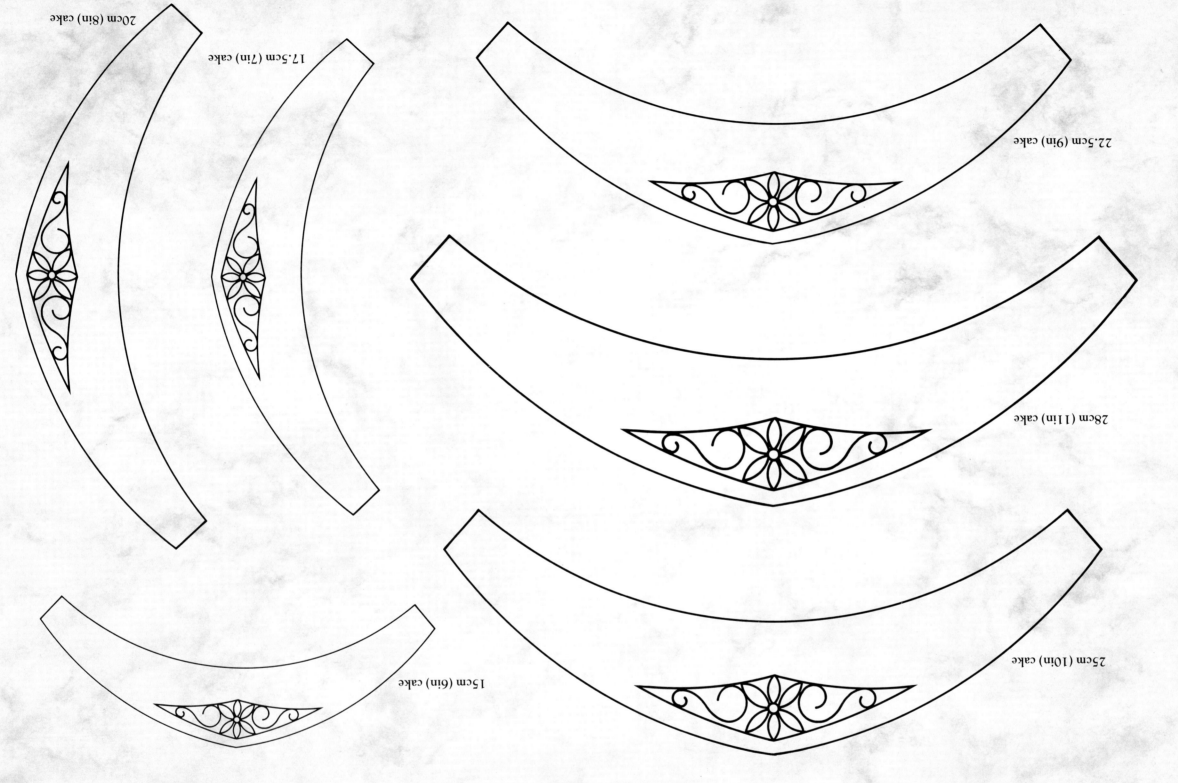

How to pipe a floral runout collar

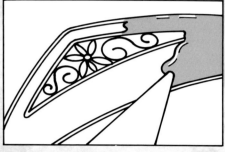

Place a piece of waxed paper over the design and outline using royal icing and a No1 tube (nozzle).

Pipe in the flower and leaf design using various coloured royal icings with fine tubes (nozzles).

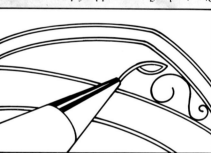

Complete the piping as shown, ensuring that the floral design is then attached to the runout collar.

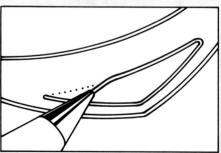

Following the piped outline, neatly flood-in using run-icing. Allow to dry, then attach to the cake with a little icing.

How to make a collar with floral overlay

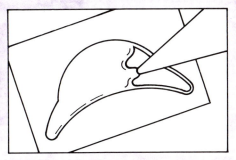

Outline and flood-in the collar shape using the same method as described on page 32. Allow to dry.

Make one floral overlay for each collar section using the same method given on page 32. Allow to dry.

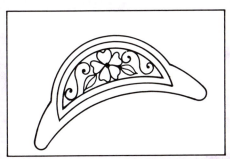

Remove the overlay from the waxed paper and position accurately onto the collar with royal icing.

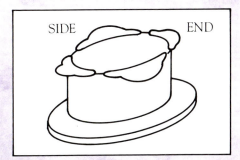

Remove the prepared collars from the waxed paper. Attach the two end collars and two side collars to the cake as shown.

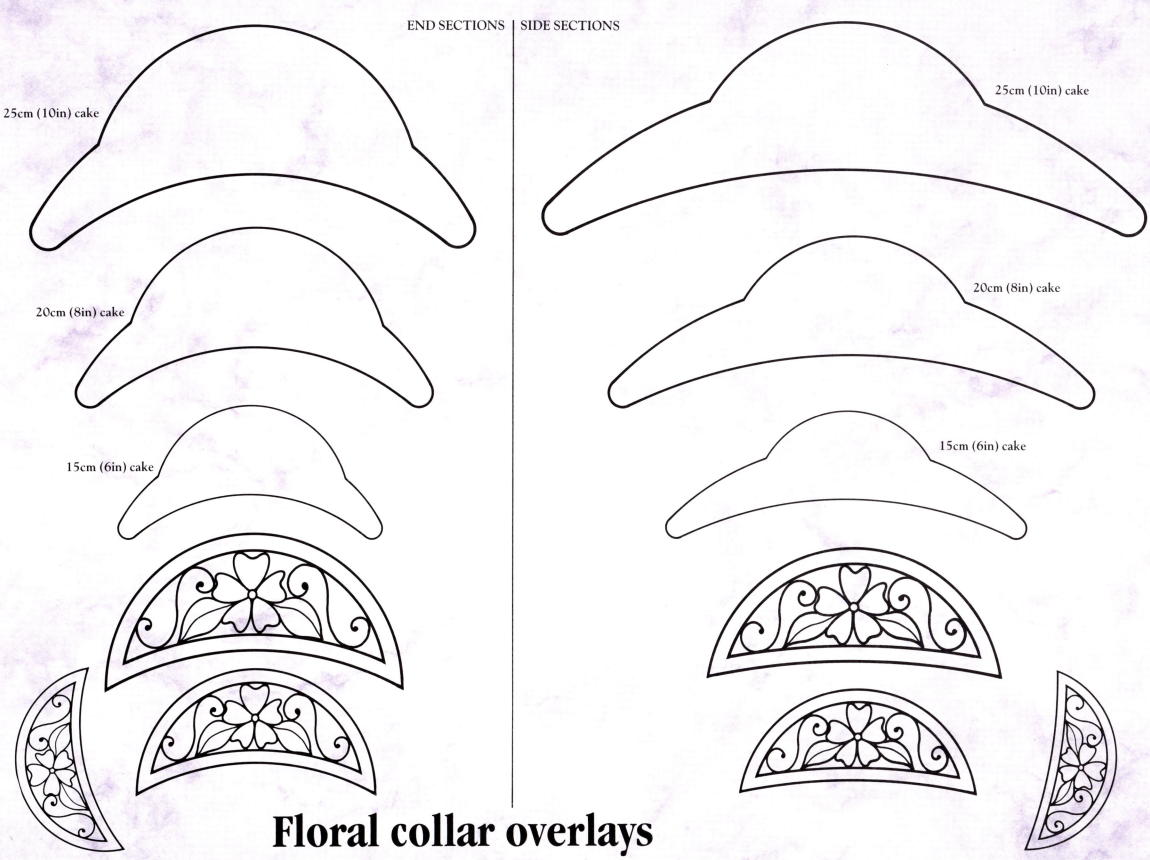

END SECTIONS | SIDE SECTIONS

25cm (10in) cake

20cm (8in) cake

15cm (6in) cake

25cm (10in) cake

20cm (8in) cake

15cm (6in) cake

Floral collar overlays

These runout collars are made using the conventional techniques described on the previous page, but have the added feature of a prefabricated section to create more interest and detail to the overall appearance. The overlay designs have been specially created with a floral theme in mind.

Four seasons

Suitable for making in more than one sugarcraft technique, here is a selection of the more popular flowers usually associated with the depiction of spring, summer, autumn and winter.

Happy Valentine

Flowers and Valentine's Day go hand-in-hand. Using the traditional heart shape as a basis for these designs, the selection covers ideas that can be accomplished in royal icing, marzipan, sugarpaste, chocolate and buttercream.

Mother's Day

Although fresh flowers are the traditional gift usually associated with this special day, a cake with edible flowers would make an equally perfect tribute. Choose from this selection of both traditional and modern designs, each suitable for more than one sugarcraft technique.

Easter flowers

Daffodils, violets, catkins and pussy willow all beautifully combined in various arrangements to provide a selection of designs suitable for Easter cakes, chocolate Easter eggs and small fancy cakes.

Christmas

The rich traditional colours associated with this festive time of year give the sugarcraft artist much scope for creating spectacular effects on their cake creations. Use greens, reds and browns in conjunction with the metallic colours of silver and gold to accomplish this array of detailed designs.

Garlands and wreaths

These garlands and wreaths could be used to form the main decoration of a cake, or reduced in size for the sides of a cake. They lend themselves to several forms of edible media and could be reproduced flat or in half relief.

Vases and baskets

An alternative to arranging flowers with just leaves and stems could be to present them in a decorative vase or basket. Many of the floral designs in the book could be adapted for use with this varied selection of containers.

40

Although not classed as flowers for cake decorating, these fungi and toadstools make nice motifs for men's cakes. The spotted toadstool (top) makes an ideal design for a child's cake. Make it red with white spots and sit a fairy or mouse beneath it!

Men's flowers

More often than not, a less-delicate type of floral decoration is required to adorn a cake made for a man. Here are a few ideas – they include pot plants, house plants, toadstools and fungi, plus designs based on gardening themes.

How to make a runout corner piece

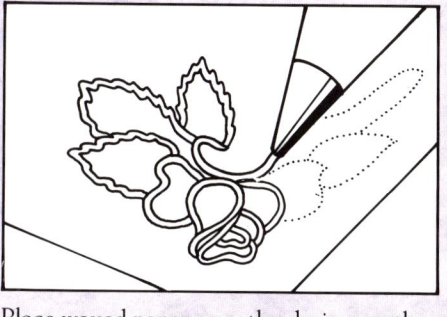

Place waxed paper over the design on the page. Outline the design using royal icing and a No1 tube (nozzle).

Flood-in the various sections with appropriately coloured run-icing. Allow to dry.

When dry, paint on detail, veins and shading using edible food colour and a fine paint brush.

Attach the finished runout corner pieces to a sugarpaste-coated or royal-iced cake.

Corner designs

These attractive floral corner pieces have been developed by the basic runout collar technique. The pieces are smaller than a corner collar, but made and applied to the cake in the conventional manner. Utilize the space between the corners to introduce linework and tiny piped border work.

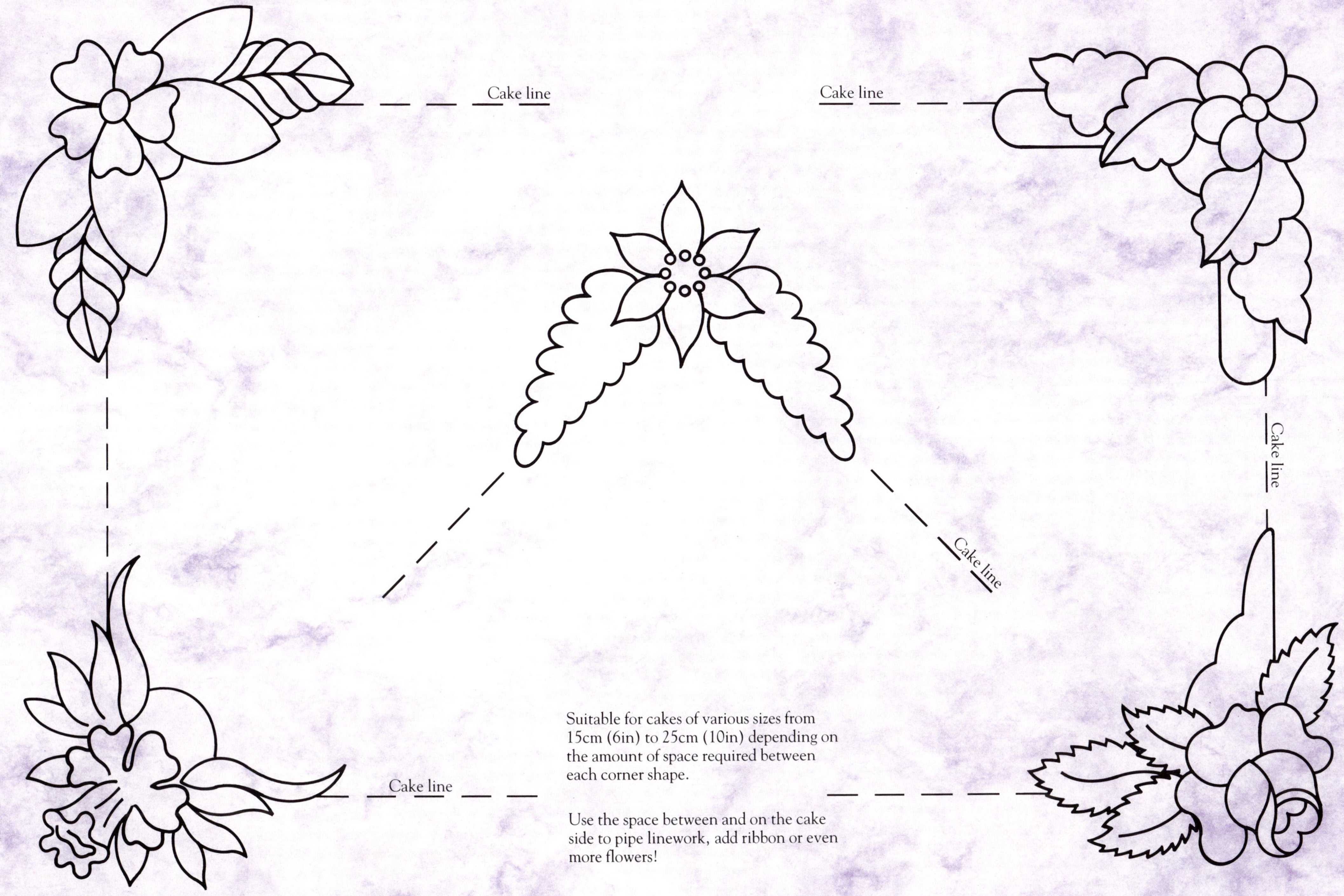

Cake line

Cake line

Cake line

Cake line

Cake line

Cake line

Suitable for cakes of various sizes from 15cm (6in) to 25cm (10in) depending on the amount of space required between each corner shape.

Use the space between and on the cake side to pipe linework, add ribbon or even more flowers!

How to stencil flowers

Select your design, trace onto oiled stencil card or thin card and cut out using a sharp craft knife.

Using the first finger and thumb, hold the prepared stencil firmly in place on the cake top or plaque.

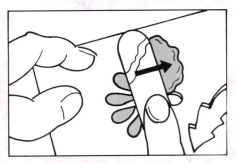

Spread coloured royal icing or buttercream over the cut-out parts using a small bladed palette knife, then remove the stencil.

Built-up flowers
Stencil petals onto waxed paper and allow to dry. Remove and assemble as shown. Pipe a centre bulb with royal icing to secure. (Petal shapes bottom right of page.)

Flowers for stencilling

Stencils provide a quick, easy and accurate method of applying designs to cake tops and sides. Here are a selection of floral designs ready for you to prepare a stencil from – as shown. The designs could also be stencilled onto prepared plaques which are then attached to a cake.

Petal shapes for built-up flowers

Use these shapes as leaves or petals to form flowers. For petals – the shapes above can be used with the pointed end in to the centre of the flower or facing outwards.

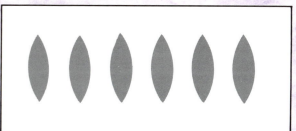

Floral lettering

Use this delicately adorned lettering with floral embellishments to complement other floral decoration on your cake. A few examples of the more popular greetings are provided, together with the alphabet to allow you to construct your own inscription or name.

Merry Christmas

Happy Anniversary

Happy Birthday

Best Wishes

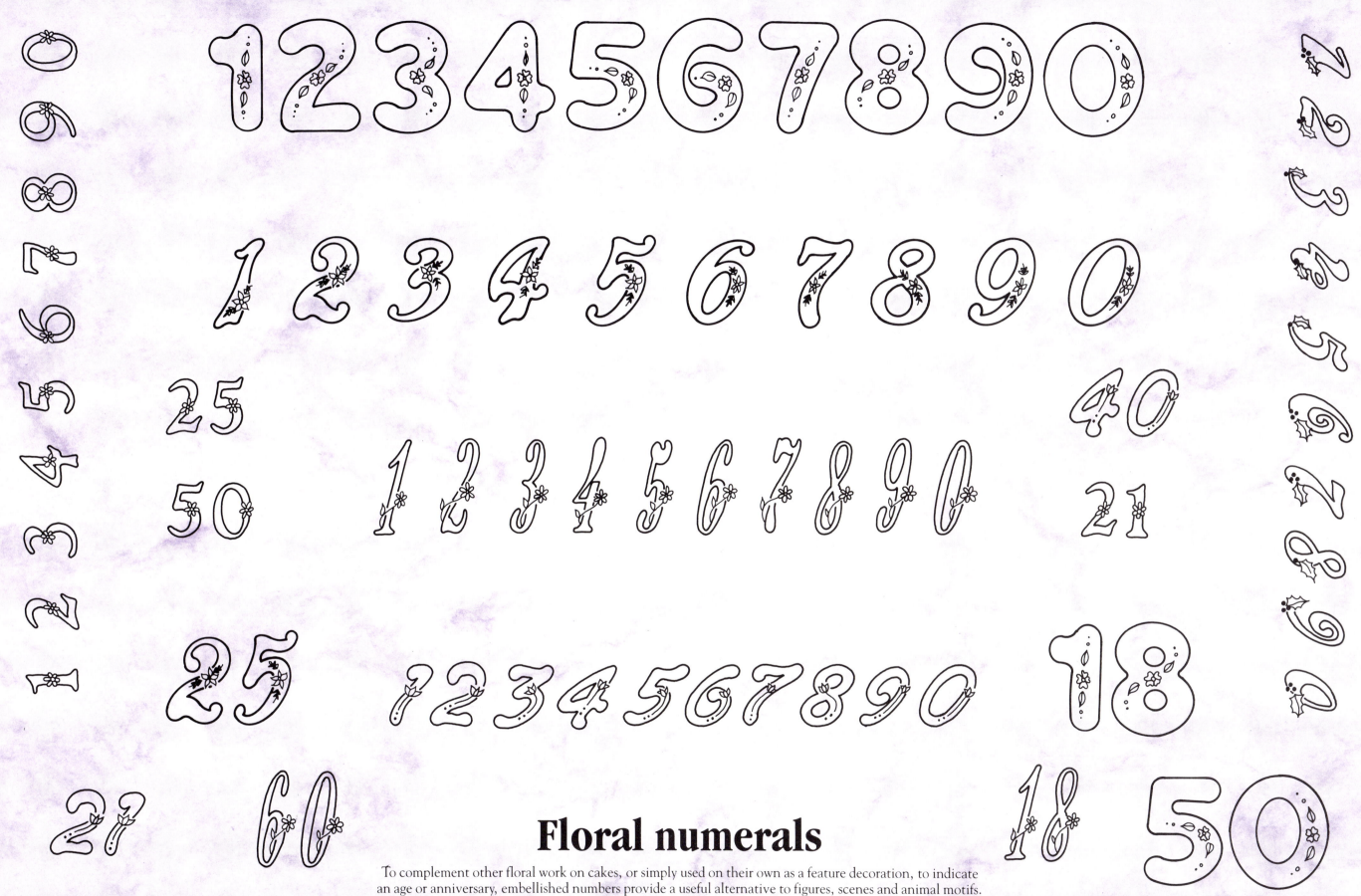

Floral numerals

To complement other floral work on cakes, or simply used on their own as a feature decoration, to indicate an age or anniversary, embellished numbers provide a useful alternative to figures, scenes and animal motifs.

45

Flower faces

Bring a smile to a child's face by using these delightfully amusing figures to decorate birthday cakes for the young ones! The ideas are suitable for more than one sugarcraft technique and various edible media.

How to pipe buttercream flowers

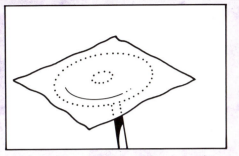

Prepare a flower (rose) nail for piping by attaching a small square or circle of waxed paper with a dab of buttercream.

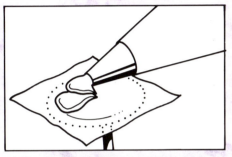

Pipe individual petals onto the paper, rotating the nail as you work. Use coloured buttercream and a petal tube.

To create pointed petals, such as daffodils and narcissi, taper each petal to a point using a moistened fine paint brush.

Pipe a bulb of coloured buttercream in the centre, then pipe small dots or spikes to represent stamen, using a fine tube.

Basic blossom

 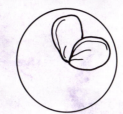   

Violet

Daisy

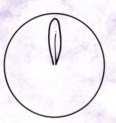    

Primrose

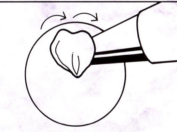 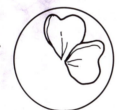 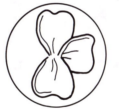  

Daffodil

How to pipe buttercream leaves

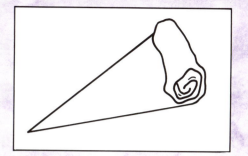

Bought leaf tubes (nozzles) can be used. To make a leaf piping bag, fill a paper piping bag with green buttercream.

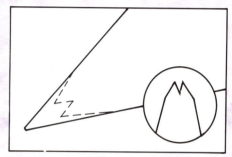

Using scissors, cut a 'W' shape at the point of the bag. The further away from the point you cut, the wider the leaves.

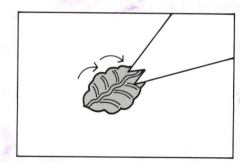

Apply even pressure during piping and move slowly, making a jerking movement gently up and down for side leaf veins.

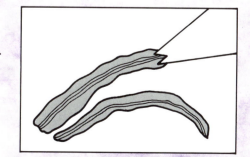

To make narrow or wider leaves, move the bag along with an even pressure. Pull the bag away for a pointed end.

Buttercream flowers

Buttercream flowers are quick and easy to make. Here are some examples of the more popular flowers using this versatile medium. Follow the step-by-step drawings as you pipe. Store them in the refrigerator until required.

Buttercream designs

Use the flowers and leaves described on the previous page to decorate your buttercream specials! Make the flowers easier to handle by removing them from the waxed paper straight from the refrigerator. Stems and leaves can be piped directly onto the buttercream-covered cake, if preferred.

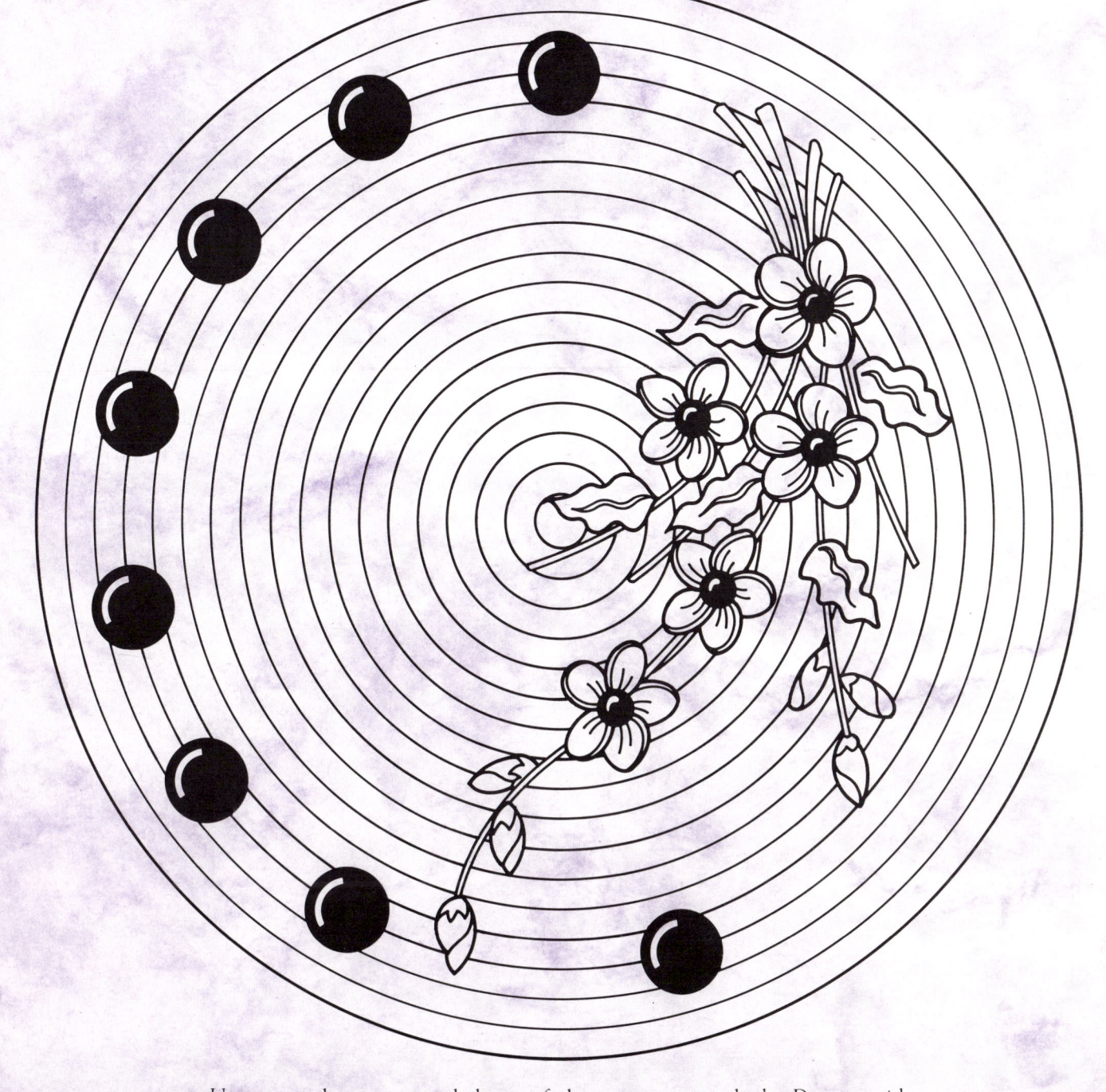

Use a serrated scraper to comb the top of a buttercream-covered cake. Decorate with flowers, leaves and chocolate drops.

Here are 12 designs for decorating buttercream cakes. Select one design and repeat on each individual segment of your cake.